Through My Eyes
A Life of Poetry and Prose

Zebulon Vance Brooks

1

zeb_brooks@yahoo.com

ISBN: 978-0-578-01603-0

Printed in the U.S.A.

Dedication

In memory of my little brother, Robert Wallace Powell
(May 17, 1978 – September 19, 2003)
You will never be forgotten. RIP.

Robert W. Powell

Acknowledgements

Thank you Lord for being there for me through the trials and tribulations of life
You lead me through the concrete jungles in the midst of the rain and the strife
You renew my spirit on the road to redemption for you are the guide of my life
And when I travel down the dark and bumpy roads of existence, I will have faith always
Your presence eases my soul
You prepare me for the war of the spirit and strengthen me in my hour of need
Your love for me shall follow me all my days and my soul belongs to you always

I want to thank my beautiful wife, Anitra Brooks, for the love and encouragement in writing this book.

Special Lady

Once every so often,
  A ray of sunshine comes to brighten my day
  It is special and unique in every way
Once every so often,
  A thunderous roar could be heard from the rain
  Many times bringing sadness and pain
Once in a life time,
  I come across a lady who is in my thoughts and mind
  A lady who is special and kind
You have become my ray of sunshine, that special lady that blocks away the thunderous roar of the rain

I also want to thank my daughters: Zaynah, Ayana, and Jada for their love and inspiration. I want to thank my Mama, Gloria Brooks, for being a strong black woman in my life. I want to thank my sister, Yolanda E. Williams (a.k.a. Baby Girl), for putting this book together. Thank you so much, Baby Girl.

Special Thanks:

Sean Brooks and family, John "The Barber" Powell, Nicole Powell, Carolyn Jean Powell, LaVonne Sauls, Shawn Stradford, Anthony Burton, Eugene Brown, family in Roxboro and Raleigh, North Carolina, family in Macon, Georgia (Unionville Community), Reid Temple AME Church Family, my family in Washington, D.C. (a.k.a. Chocolate City) and many other relatives and friends.

Rest In Peace:
Robert W. Powell, Ellis W. Brooks, Wallace Brooks, Wilma Brooks, Zebulon Vance Woods, Emily "Daisy" Woods, Daniel Carswell, Mattie Carswell (Big Ma), Thomasine Burrell (Granny), Gwen Carswell, Donald Carswell, Phillip Carswell, Iris Baird, Matrice Davis, Katherine and Theodore Lawson, Zebulon Vance Woods Jr., Nathaniel Woods, Edna Walker, Cora Dickey and Sherlock "Dean" Smith.

Contents

- Through My Eyes (pg 58)

THE DARKEST HOUR: JUDGEMENT DAY

Tick Tock, Tick Tock

Tick Tock, Tick Tock

Like sand in an hourglass, time is running out

Tell me, should I get my life in order

or

Should I continue my path on the same route?

Tick Tock, Tick Tock

Tick Tock, Tick Tock

The Day of Judgment is near

Get your mind right

The Day of Judgment is near

Get your heart right

The Day of Judgment is near

Get your soul right

Tick Tock, Tick Tock

Tick Tock, Tick Tock

Time has run out

The Day of Judgment is here

Standing at the gates of Heaven,

Angels begin to appear

The Day of Judgment is here!!

The Day of Judgment is here!!

In my darkest hour, I shall have no fear for God is with me

always

The Day of Judgment is here and

Through the midst of the gates, the face of God appears

(God Speaks)

The time has come and Judgment Day is here

Tell me about your life and what you hold dear

Why should I open my gates and let you in here?

Living in the fast lane a big part of my life

Parties, Drugs, Alcohol you can say I was full of strife

Running with the devil was a big part of me

Blinded by his wicked ways I could not see

or maybe I could see but didn't want to change that part of me

I have had many battles within the war of my spirit

The knowledge to do the right thing and be at one with you

The knowledge to do my thing and be at one with Satan

During my battles, I've lost quite a few along the way

not knowing if it would cost me in the end on Judgment Day

The Day of Judgment is here and I really don't know what to say

For my life is like a war with constant battles everyday

Today is my chance to explain why I should get the key

How can I - when most of my life has been about me, me, me

In my darkest hour, I'm starting to have doubts and fear

for the question was asked, *"What do you hold dear?"*

Knowing that the kingdom and all the riches of heaven were near

In my heart I still wasn't clear

I thought about the question that God asked me at the gate

Hoping time had not run out and that I wasn't too late

So I began to answer the question and analyze my life

All I could think about was my daughters and wife

Love is the key to open the gate

for without love how could I conquer hate?

The gates of heaven opened for me on this brand new day
It was no longer dark on Judgment Day

SUNSHINE IN THE RAIN

Have you ever seen the sun shine on a rainy day?

(Think about it)

Lights out and the heat cut off

No money for bills and can barely make it

The refrigerator is low and the hunger pains are high

No money for bills and can barely make it

 Depressed and saddened by my everyday existence

No money for bills and can barely make it.

… (Knock, Knock)

Who is it?

It's your buddy Jack Daniels.

How about a drink for old times?

I can bring you sunshine on a rainy day

No money for bills; you don't say

Can barely make it through another day

Take a drink and stop feeling this way

… (Knock, Knock)

Who is it?

It's your girl Mary Jane.

I heard you were down and feeling some pain

Frustrated with life and going insane

Can't find the sunshine in the midst of the rain

Let me see if I can straighten out this mess

Relieve you of your burdens and stress

Come on!! Take a couple of puffs and pass

You'll see the pain won't last.

…I'm feeling so good and high

My head above the clouds and in the sky

I'm feeling so good and high

I have my friends here who came by

I'm feeling so good and high

No worries, no stress I wonder why

I'm feeling so good and high

No more thoughts of suicide and trying to die…

…(Knock, Knock)

Who is it?

The Almighty, the Creator of heaven and earth.

It is I who can make the sun shine on a rainy day

It is I who have been with you since the first day

It is with Me your life can be less stress

It is with Me you can find true happiness

It is with Me you'll feel good and high

You don't need the liquor and drugs to get you by

Frustrated with life and going through pain

Trust in My Word and the kingdom you'll gain

It is I who has always been there

Open your heart to receive my care.

I've come by many times for you to let me in

Just like the prodigal son, I'm with you 'til the end.

Who is it knocking at your heart you may say?

It is I who can make the sun shine on a rainy day.

THE POWER OF GOD

The power of God is more amazing than I can imagine.

Reflecting on the darkest hour of my life,

I really don't know how to put into words the unexplainable power of God.

To be shaken to the core of your very essence,

God does things to test your faith to see if you truly believe His power.

You always hear the saying, *'You walk by faith and not by sight.'*

For sight is easy to believe in because it is right before your eyes,

while walking in faith is much different because you can not see it.

You can feel it in your heart and soul if you believe in the power of God.

Since the sudden lost of my little brother, there is not a day that goes by that I don't think of him.

As I sit here writing my thoughts down, holding back the tears,

I think of the good times we shared.

I have learned through Rob to live life to the fullest.
Anybody that truly knew Rob, knew he lived life to the fullest.

Whatever he set out to do, he did it.

Reflecting back on September 18, 2003,

I thank God for giving me one last opportunity to spend with my brother.

I remember laughing, joking, and playing Madden.

I remember saying I need to get home before I get caught out here in this Hurricane.
I remember him saying, *"You'll be alright, it's not that bad."*

I remember saying, *"I'll see you tomorrow if it's not flooded too bad."*…
(Not knowing this would be the last time I would see him alive again.)

From September 19 to September 25 I was in tremendous pain.

I hadn't felt like this ever in my life.

Constantly praying to God to take the pain away and

leaning on my family and looking to God for answers.

Believe me when I say God does answer prayers.

On September 25, 2003 I was blessed to witness the birth of my second daughter…

Ayana Celeste Brooks, a.k.a. A.C.

Reflecting back to September 24, 2003…

…I can remember getting ready to hit the road for North Carolina.

When I received a call from my wife – *"It's time"*.

I can remember while at the hospital I was thinking -

If she comes soon I can still make it to North Carolina.

I'll drive through the night.

(Not knowing God had other plans for me)
I can remember going from day to night,

now going into the AM hours of September 25, 2003.

I'm still thinking I can make it to North Carolina if she comes soon.

(Not knowing God had other plans for me)

I finally realized that I wouldn't be making it to North Carolina.

At 7:20 am with the sunlight creeping through the blinds,
I witnessed Ayana coming into the world.

For some reason I felt Rob's presence in the room during this time.

God does answer prayers.

This was the first time I didn't feel pain on the inside in about a week.

On this day God wanted me to see the miracle of life

and not the sadness and sorrow of death.

I recently received a picture with the words inscribed, 'A baby is God's way of saying – *The world should go on...*'

In my heart I feel A.C. is forever linked with my little brother Rob.

You are truly missed and never forgotten.

IN THE EYE OF THE STORM

It's sunny and bright

All seems well

All seems to be alright

Not knowing a storm is coming my way

to change lives in every way.

No longer will the norm come with the storm

No longer will life be the same

Keep the faith and continue to believe in Me.

I know you are hurting

I know you are in pain, but believe Me

the storm will pass one day

My God I'm calling out to you right now

Sometimes the pain I have is too big for me to bear

Sometimes I feel life is so unfair

I know that it is selfish for me to feel this way

Knowing there are others who suffer loss each day

In the eye of the storm is where you can find my life

Taking the good with the bad is a part of life

Continue to trust and believe in Me

You honor love ones lost by living your life

I've blessed you with two beautiful daughters and a wife

Sadness and pain will pass one day

Trust in me to show you the way

Now is not the time to be lifted

and high

Thinking this will solve your problems

and get you by

The next generation is watching everything you do,

believe me they can be worse than you

Seeing death and seeing how things could be,

how could you not have your trust in Me?

If you believe you can achieve

Many more storms will head your way

Weather the storm and you'll be okay

Misty blue is predicted in the forecast

As I reminisce on times of the past

I remember the good times with Rob on this day

The memories I have will never go away

I have your name tattooed on my arm till my dying day.

And when it's my time for my body to rest

and my soul takes flight

I hope I'm flying with Jesus like my brother Rob did

on that stormy night

MY BROTHER WILL FOREVER BE CONNECTED WITH MY DAUGHTER AYANA. THE DAY SHE CAME INTO THE WORLD WAS THE DAY THEY BURIED MY BROTHER IN NORTH CAROLINA. REST IN PEACE ROBERT WALLACE POWELL.

SOUL SISTERS

Oh how I love my soul sisters

Oh how I love my soul sisters

My soul sisters come in many shades

from dark to light and held in high regards in God's sight

Oh how I love my soul sisters

Oh how I love my soul sisters

My soul sisters are the rock and the foundation of the black family

Let's take a pen journey into the life of my soul sisters

Imagine way back in ancient times when my soul sisters were Queens!

During that time Queens spread throughout all lands in Africa...

That's right!!

Africa

The mother of civilization

The birthplace of a man

The Genesis, the beginning
A time when our soul sisters were able to live free and be the foundation of civilization

Oh how I love my soul sisters

Oh how I love my soul sisters

Imagine going back to a time when my soul sisters were shackled, chained, and taken from their family

Forced to partake in a journey to foreign lands

all at the mercy of the slave master's hands

God please have mercy on my soul!!

God please have mercy on my soul!!

(the cry of my sisters)

Forced to survive the one-way passage

Never to return home

Never to return home

Many of my soul sisters choosing death over slavery

While others journey on…

fighting disease, illness, and starvation on slave ships to the new land

Oh how I love my soul sisters

Oh how I love my soul sisters

Imagine my soul sisters arriving in the new land

No longer queens

No longer treated human

No longer free

All part of the slave master's plan

Imagine my soul sisters being whipped, beaten and raped

while the slave handlers calling them apes

Many faced to bear the seeds of the oppressor man

Work the fields; cultivate the land

all at the mercy of the slave master's hands

Crack! Crack! Crack!

(These are the sounds heard across her back)

Many dying during the process of abuse and cruelty

For four hundred years God could see my sisters' tears

For four hundred years God could see my sisters' fears

God please have mercy on me!

God please have mercy on me!

(This is the cry of my soul sisters)

I want to go home where I'm able to be free

Free from the mercy of the slave master's hands

Free from the mercy of living in everyday existence

Oh how I love my soul sisters

Oh how I love my soul sisters

Imagine a place and time when my soul sisters were on the front
line

Chosen by God to lead the way so others may see a brighter day

Harriet Tubman was her name

Freeing slaves was the game

Risking her life so others may be free

She was definitely not about me, me, me

Strong willed and fearless of man

Always determined to get the upper hand

A great soldier in the army of God

She will always be remembered throughout generations in high regards

Oh how I love my soul sisters

Oh how I love my soul sisters

Thank you Mama for your strength and courage

A God fearing woman in the eyes of God

So many sacrifices for the sake of family

Doing what you can to help the next man

You've shown me how to be a better man

A mother, father, and friend is what you have been to me

My love for you is unconditional as you can see

Oh how I love my soul sisters

Oh how I love my soul sisters

To all my single sisters trying to raise a child on your own

Remember you're not alone

When things seem bad and you feel people don't care

Look to God in prayer

Your back is against the wall and it's a struggle to make it

through the day

God is with you each step of the way

Oh how I love my soul sisters

Oh how I love my soul sisters

Thinking of my daughters and soul sisters of the present and

past…

It's a constant reminder that God's love will never pass

Oh how I love my soul sisters

Oh how I love my soul sisters

The rock of the Black family

MILITARY MINDED

No time for fear, the war is near
No time for fear, the war is near

All God's soldiers prepare for war,
It's time to take out Satan and even the score

Satan's wicked ways have been going on far too long
Time to get together and stop singing the same old song

Time for all recruits to take the oath:
I pledge allegiance to God's Army
Under the entire Kingdom of Heaven
On God's word, in which it stands
One army under God
For salvation and eternal life for all

No time for fear, the war is near
No time for fear, the war is near

Who is the enemy in this war?

Satan is the enemy we're looking to kill
God said it, it's his will

This time we will leave no enemy behind

That includes sloth, gluttony, lust, greed, envy, anger, and pride
No where to run, No where to hide

Your reign on Earth has come to an end
You had to know you couldn't win
You had to know that you weren't the most high
For your entire life is based on a lie

Destroying many souls along the way
Hoping they won't make it on Judgment Day

Filling souls with dreams you can never fulfill…
with the mark of the beast called Dollar Bill

Promising joy and happiness till the end of time,
swearing it wouldn't cost a dime

Death was destined for Satan from the start
for God knew he had no heart

Satan has a clan to spread out through foreign lands -

The message of hate and destruction to all,
The illuminati counsel is what they are called

Wars and rumors of war are at an all time high
leaving the people saying my, my, my

God please help this troubled world if you can
rid it of the wicked ways of man

God Speaks:
In order for that to happen Satan has to go,
take his life so he will exist no more
Load up them scriptures from the good Book
Satan's here, Look!! Look!!
Hit him with John 3:16 to get him shook!! shook!!
Let him feel the blood of My son,
to let him know who's the true chosen one
For Satan is a fallen angel from out the sky,
spending time on Earth trying to get by
Taking many souls as he can to the pit of hell,
this is the war of the spirit can't you tell.

This won't be easy God, for the enemy knows me well
 I was once a recruit for the gates of hell

I realized that God is the most high,
for when I pray I look to the sky

Satan has no power over me!!! Satan has no power over me!!

IS SATAN THE SON OF GOD

Is Satan the son of God who was kicked out of heaven?
If so, could he return home like the prodigal son?

We are taught that God knows all, so he had to know his favorite
angel would fall

Left in a foreign land to roam; now knowing he could never go
home

Satan is on a time clock

God is everlasting

Is Satan the son of God who was kicked out of heaven?
If so, could he return home like the prodigal son?

We are taught that God is the father to all, including you and I

So if this is true, Satan must be his son too

So what made him decide heaven wasn't good enough and that
he wanted to be the man,

with his mission to take as many souls as he can

Satan is now the king of his throne

Earth is now his new home

A place for him and his demons to roam

Satan was an angel created by God, with so much potential and
held in high regards

His outer covering was made of topaz, diamond, onyx, sapphire,
emerald, and gold…is how the story is told

Satan is a liar
So if you believe in him you will be tossed into the lake of fire

Satan knows his time is near, that's why he plays on your
emotions and what you hold dear

Is Satan the son of God who was kicked out of heaven?
If so, could he return home like the prodigal son?

The war is coming soon that will seal Satan's fate,
for he wants to be God but has too much envy, jealousy, and hate

He wanted to overtake God for the kingdom and the power

Thinking it was his time to shine in the new hour

Satan has a posse of demons waiting to recruit new souls for hell

For he knows when it comes to the final war in the end he will
fail

So the question I must ask...

Can Satan go to God and ask for forgiveness and hope He
doesn't seal his fate, or has too much time passed and now it's too
late?

Reflections on the poem:

Let me breakdown the poem - Is Satan the Son of God? The
poem is not in the literal sense. You have to think deeper than
that when you read my work. Would you agree that there is
good and evil that exists in every individual? It is up to us to
choose to follow the path of God, or to do our own thing; which
is not in alignment with God's will for our life. There was a time
in my life where I did my own thing and not the will of God. I
know Satan is not the son of God, but an angel created by God.
Now after Satan had me for 12 plus years of my life, I am asking
God can He forgive me for the wrong I did in life. I grew up in

29

the church, but along the way I got away from God. So when I ask the question at the end of the poem, I was talking about myself. I am asking God to forgive me for not doing his will and for allowing Satan to take over my life. I am asking God if I can return home like the prodigal son. As long as you come with a pure heart to God, I believe He can forgive because Jesus paid the ultimate sacrifice for our sins with his blood.

IN GOD'S PLAN FROM THE START

Out of the darkness and into the light

From the womb to the world, now I have sight

2-23 was the day I was born

The angles in heaven begin to sound their horn

The sound was so loud it traveled deep into the gates of hell that

day, bringing Satan out and looking my way

Look here, another soul to take from man,

not knowing I was in God's Plan

There have been many people that have passed before me with

such great potential and taken in their prime...

So the question I must ask God, *"What is the plan for me and*

why isn't it my time?"

My son I have plans for you bigger than you could see,

Imagine the possibilities if you just put your faith and trust in Me

So was it God's plan that I lose my father at the early age of

seven, and all they would tell me is that he went to heaven

Trails and tribulations are a part of the plan,

knowing this will help you understand

God does things we can't explain

like joy, happiness, misery, and pain

Thinking of the misery and pain that happens in life everyday

helps me to appreciate the joy and happiness sent my way

Is death the ending to life's long journey? If so, am I ready?

DEATH MUST BE EASY

NO MORE WORRIES

NO MORE STRESS

NO LONGER LIFE BEING A MESS

I'm 32 years old and I still don't know the plan,

God please help me understand

*You knew the plan all along, but you followed Satan and
continued to do wrong. Remember in the beginning Satan said,
"Here's another soul to take from man" and I told you then you
were in My plans, but you continued the worldly ways of man.
The plan is for you to be a shining example for Me and to let
others in the world witness the power of Me. In order to become
molded into a better man, trials and tribulations are a part of the
plan.*

MY THOUGHTS

Back down memory lane is where this story starts

There are a lot of things on my mind, so I'll tell it from my heart

I can remember the best of times

I can remember the worst of times

God knows my heart and feels my pain

My life is out of focus, living in the fast lane

Looking back on the time when my daddy died

Too young to remember the sadness

Too young to remember if I cried

What's up Pops? How are things in the after life?

Your oldest son is doing good

I have three daughters and a wife

Sometimes I wish you were here to see the man I am

Other times I'm full of anger and I really don't give a damn

I hate the fact that you are not here for this part of my life

Especially when there are times I just need some fatherly advice

Sometimes I wonder if you are in heaven

Living in peace, or living in hell

A place where things are never well

I hope I make it to heaven for I've seen a lot of hell

I've seen the lake of fire and Satan as well

I hope I don't go to hell for I've seen a glimpse of heaven

My daughters, Zaynah, Ayana, and Jada are all gifts from heaven

My heart and mind are always in a constant struggle to stay

focused on God

No wonder why I will never reach my full potential or stay in

high regards

There must be a reason why God still has me here,

For what reason, I'm still unclear

I just thank God for life and everything I hold dear

These are some thoughts that I have on my mind

These are some thoughts I'll seek answers to find

It's been over two years since my "little brother" died

Sometimes I feel like a piece of me died

This was my brother from a different mother

We were cousins but acted more like brothers

I miss you man and I'm saying it from the heart

As I try to recollect my thoughts, I don't know where to start

WHY THIS? WHY NOW?

It wasn't suppose to be this way

You were suppose to be around 'til we were old and grey

Now I think about my brother through my thoughts and my pen

Until I see him on the other side in the end

These are some thoughts that I have on my mind

These are some thoughts I'll seek answers to find

God sees something in me that I can't see for myself

It has nothing to do with material things, money, or wealth

Can a sinner like me be a part of God's Plan?

I hear a little voice saying, *"You can do it! Yes, you can."*

These are some thoughts that I have on my mind

These are some thoughts I'll seek answers to find.

My thoughts . . .

LIVING IN THE LAST DAYS

Black on Black violence at an all time high

The AIDS epidemic in our communities at an all time high

Babies having babies at an all time high

Mothers forced to be fathers too, Oh My!

You have rape, drugs, and murders at an all time high

Single parenthood at an all time high

Kids killing kids at an all time high

Mothers going to God asking for the reason why

They say we're living in the last days

Get your house in order and change your ways

I say we living in the last days

Get your house in order and change your ways

Countries going to war in the name of God

Countries going to war to protect their land

Revealed in Revelations across the burning sand

Unprotected sex with multiple partners

And down low brothers are increasing at a high rate

Self-genocide to our community is sealing our fate

A generation clouded by weed

Many of our youths no longer read

Parents no longer discipline or lead

Things are getting worse, yes indeed

After 400 years of enslavement

Slavery has returned in a new form

No longer are slave masters with whips and chains

Now you have big corporations building more prisons than schools

Judges handing down maxed out time to browns and blacks

For the selling of cocaine in the form of crack

Preachers no longer preaching about prophets

Preachers now preaching for profits

Preachers no longer feed the needy

Preachers now fatten their pockets and try to be greedy

Give freely to me for a better life

Oops, I mean to give to God for a better life

Time is close to running out for all

Like the change in seasons from summer to fall

Time is close to running out for all

I'll be a soldier in God's army standing tall

Satan's reign on Earth will end

For we all must stand at the foot of the throne in the end

WORDS OF WISDOM

To my daughters and nieces, don't get caught in a man's trap

For most men lie with their words and rap

Believe me when I say it's a trap

For most boys and men lie with their words and rap

Save yourself for marriage is an easy thing to say,

but reality is that I didn't go about it that way

Sometimes I would lie and say anything they wanted to hear

just to get to their very essence and what they valued to be dear

I love you/do you love me? We should come together as one.

Not knowing it's a trap and I'm just trying to have fun

I have connected with many that I promised to be my wife,

knowing it was a lie.

You can say I was trifling…

Taking your very essence was a game I liked to play

Not knowing it would come back on me one day

Now I have 3 daughters and nieces whom I tell about men's lies,

so they don't have to go through the cycle of hurt, misery, and

cries

Your body is a temple and your essence a gift from God,

so please don't take my words lightly in this regard

To my daughters and nieces, don't get caught in a man's trap

For most men lie with their words and rap

Believe me when I say it's a trap

For most boys and men lie with their words and rap

When you connect with someone in that special way,

be ready for the consequences sent your way

Every person you sleep with, you are forever connected in life

Even if you become someone else's wife

It's not a game when you give of yourself so free

For in return you might receive a unwanted pregnancy

I say it's not a game when you give of yourself so free

For in return you might receive a disease known as HIV

CORNER BOY BLUES

Standing on the corner with my drugs and a gun

Chilling' with my boys and trying to have fun

I'm just a kid lost in the world of dope

and I can't see any way out or hope

That's corner boy blues

Stick up boys waiting to take my bread

They pull out a gun...Click...I'm not dead

The gun jams and I begin to run fast

Trouble seems to always pop up from my past

That's corner boy blues

I have no dreams for tomorrow, for I'm living day to day

Is life really supposed to be that way?

I have no future and I'm stuck in the past

At this rate my life won't last

That's corner boy blues

I'm having sex at an early age because I think I'm the man

Trying to get through life the best way I can

I'm having unprotected sex and trying to get laid

Now I have a disease called AIDS

That's corner boy blues

I hope these young girls haven't read the poem *"Words of Wisdom"* and try to change their lives

For I'm going to sleep with as many as I can and try to take their lives
That's community blues

Now I have this gun to my head

As I begin to pull the trigger...Click...I'm not dead

The gun jams and I don't hear a blast,

so I dropped to my knees and begin to pray fast

My God, My God

Why did you save my life, when I tried to end my life?

I can feel that the presence of the Lord is here

because I can feel Him in the atmosphere

My son, it is not the time for your life to end

Actually this is the time for your life to begin

You want me even though I sold dope, carried a gun, and tried to

kill young girls with my disease, and attempted to take my life?

Why God did you spare my life?

I'm considered a low life, a thug, and a gangster brother by most

in the hood

People always pointing and saying I'm up to no good

Hell's angel most would say,

so I lived up to the reputation in every way

Why God did you spare me?

I needed your spirit to be free, to let others know the powers of

ME

That even someone who is considered a low life can in fact

change their life

Thank God for sparing me

Now my soul is free

Now my soul is free

Reflection on this poem:

The "Corner Boy" represents a culmination of people I knew in my youth, showing the consequences of our actions and how we can affect others in our communities and the world.

LOOKING FOR LOVE

Lost in a sea of hopelessness and despair

Looking for love, but I don't know where

Keeping my head above water in the big blue sea

Searching for love is where you can find me

Starting to sink fast with no love in sight

I think I'm gonna drown tonight

Can't breathe and losing focus fast

Flashes of memory appear from my past

Seeing my wife for the very first time

I knew then she was more than a dime

She represents everything that is good in my life

Thank you, God for a beautiful wife

My life is full of darkness even in the light

Sometimes I just want to give up without a fight

Somehow I lost love in a sea of hopelessness and despair

Now I'm looking for love but I don't know where

Can't breathe and losing focus fast

Flashes of memory appear from my past

The birth of Zaynah is a memory I see clear

That day I will always hold dear

A beautiful baby added to my life

To go along with my beautiful wife

My first born and special in every way

A little mini me most would say

I see flashes of love

as it always come from heaven above

I'm sinking deeper in a sea of hopelessness and despair

Looking for love, but I don't know where

Can't breathe and losing air fast

Flashes of memory appear from by past

The birth of Ayana is a memory I see clear

That day I will always hold dear

So full of emotions running through me on that day

Expressions of joy and pain would not go away

Joyful for the fact I have another baby girl in my life

Painful for the fact I have lost a brother in my life

Ayana, you have a guardian angel for life

I'm sinking deeper in a sea of hopelessness and despair

Looking for love, but I don't know where

Can't breathe and losing air fast,

Flashes of memory appear from my past

The birth of Jada is a memory I see clear

That day I will always hold dear

My baby girl, the youngest in my life

Such a joy and bundle of energy added in my life

God, bless my family and keep them safe and secure

As my girls grow older and become more mature

God, look after my wife

for she is the best thing that has happened in my life

Somehow I lost love in a sea of hopelessness and despair

Now that my time is up, no need to find out where

As I journey to the other side of life

I realize love was never lost

It was buried deep in my heart

To find it, I had to do my part

Stay focused on God

Stay focused on God

Stay focused on God

are the echoes I hear clear

God is Love

God is Love

God IS LOVE is what I hold clear

Look for God and you will find love

For love comes from heaven above

SILENCE

I can see

I can see deep in your soul

I can see your hurt

I can see your misery

I can see your pain

Thoughts of suicide

Losing your mind and going insane

I can see that you hate life

Why do you feel this way?

Is it like this everyday?

Even in silence you speak aloud

You are not happy

There is a void in your heart

Silence...

SPIRITUAL INCARCERATION

Bound, chained, and shackled is where you can find my spirit

Locked up, locked down is where you can find my spirit

Satan is the warden of the prison and his demons are the guards at the gate

I didn't even have a trial and he sealed my fate

Now I'm locked away in this prison called Spiritual Incarceration

Where he wants to keep me for the next generation

Institutionalize is the goal

Where he can work on my spirit and take my soul

The warden said he wants to isolate me in my cell,

put me on death row, and sentence me to hell

How did I get locked away in this prison called Spiritual

Incarceration where he wants to keep me for the next generation?

I was destined to be great, now I'm sitting in my cell and waiting on my fate

Twenty-four hour lock down with no time on the yard

I guess that's supposed to keep me from God

I don't think Satan realize I made a call to my lawyer, Jesus, and he said - *Keep the Faith and Hold On.*

Satan made a personal visit to my cell and said - *Tonight is the night I will see you in hell.*

The guards escorted me down the hall to the electric chair

I was so full of faith that I really didn't care

Strapped to the chair with the currents on high

Tonight is the night I was supposed to die

But wait...

The phone rings in my death chamber; it's a call from the Most High

Where He tells Satan - *Release him for it's not his time to die*

Set him free, for his soul belongs to Me

I let you have him for over 12 years of his life

Now it's time to show him his purpose-driven life

I let you take him to the valley of the shadow of death

I let you take him to the lake of fire

I let you take him to jail, to show him flashes of hell

But I can't let you take his soul for it belongs to ME,

So un-strap the chair and set him free

The Holy Ghost is here to make sure everything is cool,

So Satan don't act like a fool

God...Why was I left here with no hope or desire,

for I knew all along Satan was a liar?

You were baptized by water with reaching the kingdom as your

ultimate desire

So I had to let Satan have you and put you through the fire

The Holy Ghost is here now to be a guide for your heart

Now it's time to be a witness for ME and do your part

My God!! My God!!

You have been great to me, for I'm no longer in spiritual

incarceration because you set me free

God let your will be done with the Holy Ghost leading the way

Jesus didn't even charge me, for He paid with his blood on the

cross on that special day

I'm Free!!!

I'm Free!!!

Thank God, I'm Free!!!

FACE OFF: ZEB VS ZEB

(Good Zeb Speaks)

I am a walking contradiction

There is a yin to my yang

There is good to my evil that resides in me

I am a child of God despite the fact that Satan

is recruiting me on a daily

There is a constant face off of my spirit for the

battle of my soul

God knows I want to do right, but I continue to do wrong

Making it to heaven on my mind...

Satan not far behind

Controversy looms all around me

Zeb vs Zeb is what they see

Face off must be about me

God you continue to put me through the trials and tribulations of

life, making it hard to suppress the strife

God I pray to you for wisdom and guidance

To lead my family and my life

(God Speaks)
I've given you the answers, but you wanted to live your life.

 (Evil Zeb Speaks)

I am not a walking contradiction, for anger and

negativity are the norm in my life

Strife has permanent residence in my heart

I'm in a constant battle with Good Zeb for the

possession of our soul

God knows I never want to do right and

I always want to do wrong

Strife looms all around me

Zeb vs Zeb is what they see

Face off must be about me

(Good Zeb Speaks)

Why the trials?

Why the tribulations?

Is this supposed to be the way of life?

Constantly under stress to look good and do my best

Wondering when the next storm in life

is heading my way like the rise of

Sun on a new day

I want to be the man God wants me to be

for I know it's not about me, me, me

I want to kill the evil that is taking over my life

for it's starting to destroy the kids and my wife

 (God speaks)

Stand up strong; be a husband, father, and a man

I've shown you the blueprint now

Stand up BLACK MAN!!

 (Evil Zeb Speaks)

I thrive on chaos and turbulence

I'm glad life is this way

No worries, no stress

This is when I'm at my best

Can't wait till the next storm of life

heads my way so I can unleash my strife

in everyway

Whatever God brings together I destroy it

with hate –

It doesn't matter the circumstances or my fate

I want to be the man I want to be

For everything is all about me, me, me

I'm killing the good that wants to be a part of my life

That includes my better half, my wife

(Good Zeb Speaks)

God I need you now more than ever in life

to help me lead my kids and wife

To be the man they need me to be

For the next generation is watching me

I have visions of blessings coming into my life

as long as I stay focused on God, the head of my life

God is the head of my life

Without Him there is no life

God has blessed my life in everyway

I have to thank Him everyday

Far from a perfect man,

but I still know I'm in God's Plan

I'M FREE

The spirit of the Lord is here

I can feel Him in the atmosphere

He released me from sloth
He released me from gluttony
He released me from lust
He released me from greed
He released me from anger
He released me from envy
He released me from pride

I'm no longer locked up - I'm Free!!
Thank God for saving me!

When I look back in my past, He showed me I was in His plans

from the start

He let me know then Satan had no heart

He let me know that the Holy Spirit was the sunshine on a rainy

day and if I believe, blessings will be sent my way

He showed me His power in the eye of the storm,

where things are never the norm

He showed me the love He has for my soul sisters even in the

midst of chaos

He heard my thoughts even in silence, during spiritual

incarceration

Losing focus and going insane…

to give me words of wisdom for the corner boy blues

I know Satan is not the son of God, and that God is the essence

of love

Even when I was looking for love in a sea of hopelessness and

despair, God was always right there

He showed me during my face off for my soul

that He is always in control

The gates of heaven open for me on this brand new day,

for it was no longer dark on Judgment Day

I'M FREE!!!

THROUGH MY EYES

Through my eyes I can see misery and pain
Young black youths trying to make it through the rain
Through my eyes I can see abuse and violence
Another victim trying to cope through silence
Through my eyes I can see the improper touch of little boys and girls
Another child's sense of security and innocence lost in this cruel world
Through my eyes I can see prejudice and hate
Passed down through generations to seal humanities fate
Through my eyes I can see sex before marriage
Too many young girls pushing a baby carriage
Through my eyes I can see fewer fathers in the home
Many of our young boys left in the streets to roam
Through my eyes I can see slums, ghettos, and the hood
Where many of our youth are so misunderstood
Through my eyes I can see the results of heroin and crack
Destroying many communities that are brown or black
Through my eyes I can see people who look like me
Who hate people that look like me
Through my eyes I can see genocide with no regard for life
From Rwanda to Darfur, so full of hate and strife
Through my eyes I can see Willie Lynch's philosophy has come to pass
To separate us as a people into groups and class
Through my eyes I can see we are carrying out his plans
To enslave our body, mind, and spirit across the lands
Through my eyes I carry the stripes of my ancestors across my back
For my ancestors carry the stripes of racism across their back
Through my eyes I can see a brighter day
For I'm an image of God molded in a unique and special way
Through my eyes I can see it all
That God is my all and all
Through my eyes I can clearly see that life is just not about me, me, me
Through my eyes…

Cover Art by John "The Barber" Powell

Drawing on Dedication page, Robert W. Powell, by Miss Dee of Metro Ink Tattoo

www.ingramcontent.com/pod-product-compliance
Lightning Source LLC
Chambersburg PA
CBHW022341040426
42449CB00006B/661